for Trevelyan

NOT LOST, JUST SOMEWHERE ELSE

Hazel Edwards

Illustrated by Leanne Argent

Hill of Content
Melbourne

'What have you lost this time?'

Mummy worries about things getting lost.

John
Hieu
Sue
Hope you
get better
soon xx
ANNIE
Sophie
Kim
Julie
Jill
Elleni
MATHEW
Adam.
Graham
Simon
Kerry
David

'My sneaker isn't lost.
It is just somewhere else.'

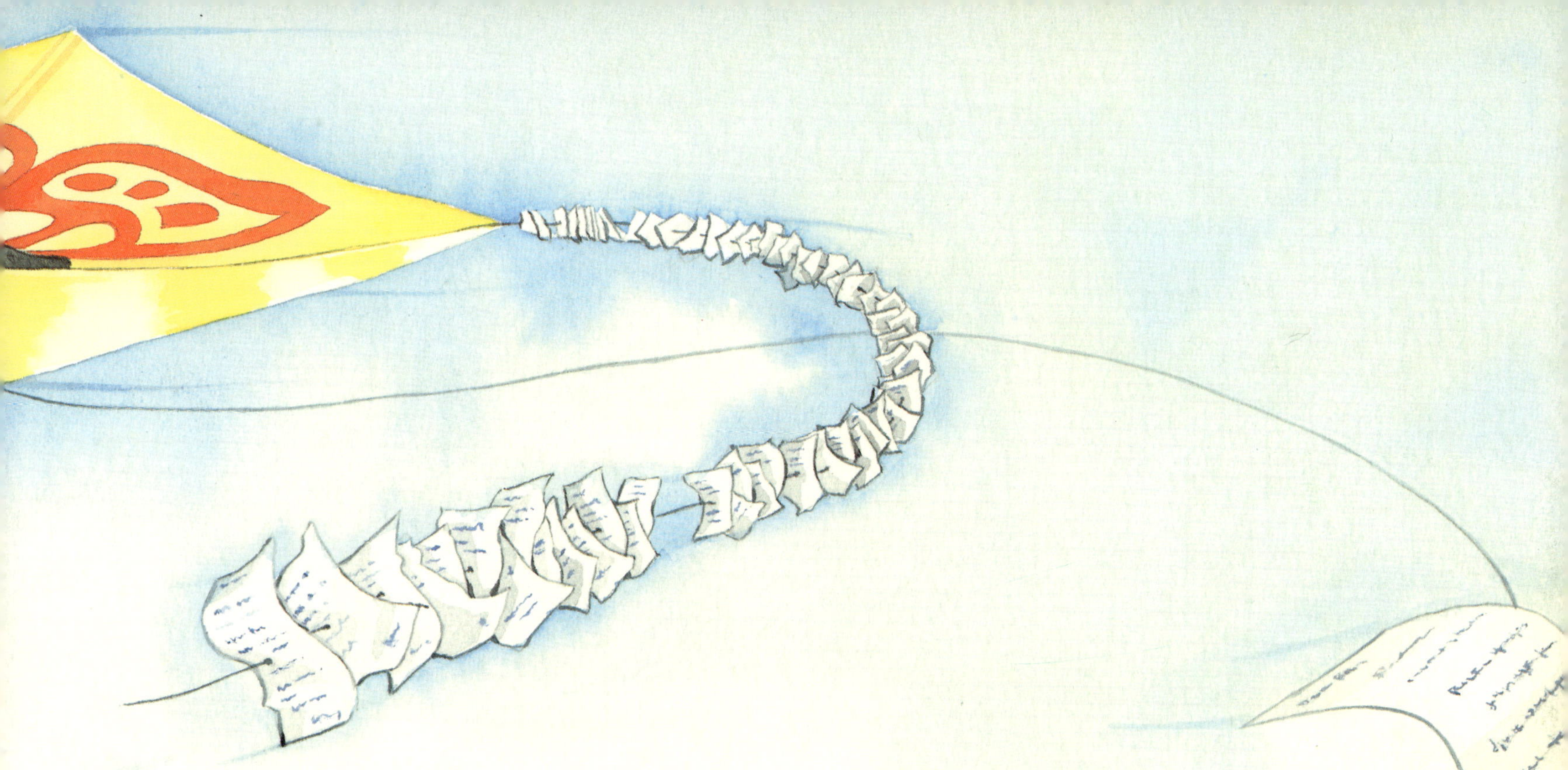

‘Where’s the note from school?’

‘Somewhere.’

Nothing is really lost.
Things are always somewhere else
more interesting.

Cats
LOS
PROPE
TAKE
CARE

‘You’d lose your head if it wasn’t screwed on,’
said my Uncle Robert who works in Railway Lost
Property.
But my head was still there.
I checked.

'Your name was on your parka.
How could you lose it?'
I didn't lose my parka.
Somebody borrowed it.

They said Uncle Robert lost his heart over his girlfriend.

But he looked the same to me.
He was still breathing.

Daddy is strict.
'Hold my hand, or you'll get lost.'
Daddy always says that.
But how can I get lost?
I'm with me.

SPECIAL

BUTCHER
FISH & CHIPS
DELI
BANK
HOTEL MOTEL
SURF LIFE SAVING CLUB

Even with his big map
in the car,
Grandpa gets lost.
But that's fun.
We go to some interesting places.

Yesterday, I took Mrs Amit's dog for a walk.
He doesn't go out much.
I came back by myself.

'Where's my dog?'
That's when Mrs Amit lost her temper.
'Have you lost Hannibal?'

But I don't lose pets.
I just leave them somewhere more interesting.

Daddy can't cook without his recipe book.
And he always makes our birthday cakes.

'Where's my cook book? Don't say I've lost it.'

We looked everywhere.
It was lost down the back of the fridge.
'Found it.'

bread
soup
tissues
battery
milk
dog food
OFFEE
BAKING CA
BAK
CAKE
COOKBOOK

JOHN
DEB

Sometimes, I get lost with me.
At the Show, the teacher said, 'Don't get lost.'
I let the police find me.
They need children to play in their police station.

Daddy's car is very important to him.
'Where are my car keys?'

He couldn't find them, so
Daddy walked to work.

His keys weren't lost.
They were in a secret place.

Sometimes people are lost.
My friend Steve lost his Grandma.
But she went somewhere.
She wasn't really lost.
And he hasn't forgotten her.

Sometimes my Gran's mind gets lost.
But she always finds me.
She doesn't mind if I lose things.
We just have a cuddle.

Gran took me to the cricket.
Our team lost the ball.
But we still played a game.
Gran can do spinners with oranges.

Saturday was Daddy's birthday.
'What's this?'
Daddy unwrapped his birthday present.
'My car keys!'
I knew he'd like his present.

Nothing is lost.
It just goes somewhere else!

Illustrator's dedication:
To Hiêũ and Kerry

First published in Australia 1990
by Hill of Content Publishing
86 Bourke Street, Melbourne 3000

Typeset by Midland Typesetters, Maryborough, Vic.
Printed in Singapore by
Welpac Printing & Packaging Pte Ltd

National Library of Australia
Cataloguing-in-Publication data

Edwards, Hazel, 1945-
Not lost, just somewhere else.

ISBN 0 85572 203 7

I. Argent, Leanne, 1964- . II. Title.

A823.3